Shadows on Moss

Shadows on Moss

Published Poetry of P. M. Flynn

P. M. Flynn

RESOURCE *Publications* · Eugene, Oregon

SHADOWS ON MOSS
Published Poetry of P. M. Flynn

Resource Publications
An Imprint of Wipf and Stock Publishers
199 W. 8th Ave., Suite 3
Eugene, OR 97401

www.wipfandstock.com

PAPERBACK ISBN: 979-8-3852-0733-6
HARDCOVER ISBN: 979-8-3852-0734-3
EBOOK ISBN: 979-8-3852-0735-0

VERSION NUMBER 01/03/24

This book is dedicated to my wife and my two, red-headed step-children. They had me at "Huh, him?" My wife had a dream about me after my hanging out in her coffee shop for three years. She completes me in more ways than I can count. (And I can usually count to over a hundred in one sitting.) Plus, she gets me, laughs at a majority of my stupid jokes.

I've been writing poetry since I was 14 years old. I did a spring cleaning a dozen years ago or so and got rid of the bad poetry and a majority of the miscellaneous idea scraps. *Shadows on Moss* is a result of the revision thrust that swept all the dust and cobwebs from my files. Just as I am not perfect, as my life reflects in some of these poems, I love God in my heart. I hope you enjoy this first collection of published poems.

Contents

Publishing Credits

Shadows on Moss First published online: July 10, 2019 theplumtreetavern.blogspot.com and later in *A New Ulster 128*, August 2023

Event Horizons in the University of Houston's *Glass Mountain, Volume 19, Fall 2017*

In the Presence of Dreams Published Online in *Pure Slush*, 29 June 2016

The Wasteland Revisited Published Online: *Heroin Chic*

Haiku Published in *50 Haikus, Volume 1, Issue 10*

Transformation of the Ovary (into Fruit) Published in *The Virginian Pilot Magazine*

Toy Animal Time in the *Helen Literary Magazine* blog, *Friday Night Lights*, Dec. 25, 2015

Evil Drives a Minivan Published in *Spillway #24*

A Girl Covered in Forest Published in *The Notebook #5, The Grassroots Women's Project*

Angels, Pearls and Mannequins, The Center of the Universe, The Ferryman's Opera and **Spirits from a Bamboo Grove** Published online in *The Fictional Café, April 2016*

Dark Pursuit first published in *Slush Verdant Truth Serum* Vol. 5 July 2020

Screw Most, If Not All MFA Programs in Issue 9, *Fleas on the Dog Online Quarterly,* 2021

Mannequins in a Perfect World Published, *CactiFur, Online* October 6, 2021

The Signs of Water, Shadows of Eternity, Under a Colored Sky and **Valentine Secrets** Published Online *Agape Review 2–24-2023*

The Nature of Seagulls Published in *Pure Slush Home Anthology* 4–2023

A Church of Days and **Islands of Eternity** appear in *The Tide Rises, the Tide Falls* online May-June 2023

A Season of Angels appeared in the December 2001, *Main Street Rag*

Uncut Maps Published in *Words & Whispers,* https://www.word-sandwhispers.org/issue-12

A Hurricane Season, A House of Rising and Falling Suns, A Letter to Delilah, One Explanation for Divorce, Road Trip and **Self-Made Self** in *BlazeVox,* Volume 23, Spring 2023

New Worlds in Moments To be published in *Straylight* Magazine, Spring 2024

Shadows on Moss

I remember these woods from a photograph of snow
around a stage; overgrown space that became forest.

Moss shadows cover the pines,
at night, as a cold shiver speaks:

pinesap hardens each winter. Branches chill.
Leaves scatter or blow downwind; sap,
like flesh and blood once captured this band
for a magazine shoot; pages yellowing
before turning brown in a closeted room.

They live in weeks past sleeves of shelved music:

before it snowed all day, on harvest fields
outside, walking over broken branches
fallen on a bowed, mildewed stage,
performance worn in the faded pictures;
old songs and melodies snapping
like frozen ice in a field; songs fading now
as the moon crosses the night sky; shadows
and moss on one side of a tree, in light
that does not meet the snow anymore.

Event Horizons

The top of trees are the horizon:

or, from heights above, forests are a longer line
curving below an edge of sky becoming dawn
or dusk where light divides a day, twice;
heart to spirit and mind to soul—this body.

Man, covered with the fleshy shell of time
and place, like a season's pecan harvest:

To crack them—a machine chain pulls each nut,
snapping shells one at a time, uncovering the life
inside; pieces breaking and falling into a hopper
with the bruised seeds blending into a bigger pile
under the metal framing of control and foundation
met on the street, in an office or break room;
life to seed, and seed to soil again; words spoken
to hearts or thoughts shared with conscience.

There, naked, seemingly flawed black spots appear
on the new skin, grown under the shell; to harden
into roots, branches drawing water to the small flesh
of smooth wrinkles tied to bare ground, that now die
after falling from the highest branch of its tree.

In the Presence of Dreams

A day's bright air fades over my shoulder
where I push all distance:

behind clouds that surround two empty chairs, ignoring
an otherwise crowded sky. I close my eyes again.

A glossy road, a dark mirror or a polished river reflects
the bright glare; light for or against a water's course,
and only at dusk when days no longer move.

For now, I follow the white lines to town:

most travelers arrive first, drafting winds from lighted streets
to darkness scattering burnt ashes on what doesn't sell
and is cast aside.

Here, in my car, I ride with any moment remembered
from inside rooms of flesh and blood, or the white static
of TV screens, the soft midnight of lace bathing any room
with more attention than is necessary.

Setting aside peripheral houselights, I pass billboards and
returning traffic, their drumming music pounding distractions

into the crammed space of cigarettes, liquor, and whatever
dreams come true while sleeping with any street or town.

At home, in the leaning of the tallest trees,
weak shadows fall on lain grass:

I sense your presence from another dream
as I walk over invisible dew cooling in moonlight.

The Wasteland Revisited

"The wild animals honor me, the jackals and the owls, because I provide water in the desert and streams in the wasteland, to give drink to my people, my chosen, the people I formed for myself that they may proclaim my praise." Isaiah 43:20–21

1. The Burial of the Dead Garbage

April Fool's is the deadliest day of the year, calling every Tom, Dick or Harry jester out of the woodwork. Like breeding termites they intermarry terror with remembrances of jokes past. Winter kept the autumn garbage from stinking up the neighborhood. Summer surprised us, the heat coming before spring this year.

After the garbage decomposed all the way we stopped wearing swimmer's nose-clips and took a picnic through the pocket-door gazebo on the lake, drank sun tea distilled from salt water spilled over filtered ice cubes, and talked about sitcoms.

I was a child once, Swiss, German, and Irish. Being the oldest I always had to take out the trash except when visiting cousins in the Midwest. Sometimes, I remembered missing the first few minutes of "The Honeymooners" because some wounded refuse bag began to crawl through the house: starting near the kitchen door and dragging itself across the battlefield screaming for a corpsman.

Spring or summer in the Corn Belt you sneeze a lot. The stalks are tall, shedding pollen, all nature ready for one big blue, harvest moon. But most of farming is excess, leavings tilled under long fields; a wayside mowed once or twice a year. What of the crop that is spirit? What new religions grow from the stony wayside? Paradise fallen on hard times boiling 10-cent bags of noodles for nourishment.

I dream of Jeannie's body, soul, and spirit: balanced before the Fall, before the Son took the garbage of life upon himself. Christmas shops cannot merchandize you. It doesn't play in Poughkeepsie. No, sir. Hell is a very small place to fall out of. No earthen garbage pit could hold you to the grave.

Poets air their dead garbage in public in the hope it will somehow live forever. For poets: hopelessness is the enemy; that and dirty old men, porn queens, and movie stars: the self-imposed, exiled dreamstuff tossed from humanity's doorsteps onto the garbage heaps of formulaic vision. Their fear of dusty, religious germs kicks at every passing wind through pulp gossip fiction recycled on afternoon talk shows during the water cooler rush of the business day.

I could not mush her perfumed breasts at our power lunch late last year. I figuratively carried her fragranced heart for over a year before she transferred to Casting.

Horrible Hagar's personal clairvoyant grossed out his relatives. A crystal ball replaced the tarot cards. His wife viewed her kin as Arian white trash, like a pack of wild dogs roaming the pages of the Sunday comic strip on Presidential search and destroy missions.

Witches eat belladonna like steroids I suppose. No personality cards for insider trading. The Dork, the man who's never invited to parties. The Nerd, who sells blood to the Red Cross to pay for surgical tape to fix glasses or buy fresh pencils and calculator batteries. There are the Idols, male and female singers who travel the world with a price on their heads, though few ever meet them in person or know if they are any more real than the sacred HD pixels they inhabit. Finally, the deathbed Psychologist takes priestly confessions at the worst possible moment. Fear eternal death in a Lake of Fire.

Universal City: so many actors and actresses have passed under your doors, rising and falling under a jet stream of publicity born from hands shaken in singing, gurgling Jacuzzis. Why doesn't anyone pick his or her nose on primetime? The networks give the public what it wants. I suppose to keep right brains holding in Slo-Mo.

"You were with me at the Oscars?"
"That dud you planted in the schedule last year. . .has it begun to sprout?"
"Do cows have magic wings?"

Millionaire Bruce Wayne became a sleaze king after syndication. Batman's ward, the Boy Wonder, died of AIDS, not into Bruce, Vicki or the sell-through.

2. A Game of Chests and Bulges

The tube chair she sat in, like a polished throne glowing beside the marble entertainment center. A dead screen comes to life at the touch of a designer button on the matching ivory control box. The HDTV with DAT premiered without litigation. Casting was impeccable. Her golden hair and Carolina Blue eyes had nothing to do with the story at hand. They tasted each other's attributes. Predictably, interruptions followed one after another for several minutes. After their moment passed, lost for all eternity, I turned to the HDTV Repair Shopping Channel to get fresh quotes.

Every window was alive in the mall. Plate glass everywhere breathed in unison with my own rising and falling chest hair. Into my own house I carted many exotic items shipped in from around the world for precisely this moment in time.

"You have learned the plastic well, young Luke," the invisible teacher whispered to his young Jedi dressed as a metallic-suited knight on October 31st.

"Is this a fraternity prank?" the cleavaged Clerk bounced out impatiently.

"I believe in the Force, God, the Creator or whatever individual preference gives you at least one unique trait so as to keep him, her, and everyone from mixing everything up," the virile Jedi offered. (Words spoken by a Jedi always hang over a crowd an extra few seconds.)

She accepted the purchase card and pressed routine keys with wide red, celluloid, and pouting lips, for the fortieth time that day. The Jedi entertained the thought he was becoming predicable in some manner, a regular customer, a statistic in some business database or hacker's memory bank. The Jedi had just spent thousands on therapy to assure humanity his minimum one, individual trait was still intact.

"The world is a mixed up enough place as it is," his beautiful, Princess Lea look-alike Bride countered.

"You are my sister and my friend; straight from Sex Ed class," the Jedi focused on her eyes.

"Can't wait for an irresponsible sex addict to keep life interesting."

"Love is a relative, beautiful thing."

The Clerk slid the Jedi's purchase into a seemingly bottomless bag along with a dozen or so, freshly inked receipts and advertising brochures. She slowly looked up and down the Jedi's rippled body while his newlywed wife stood stoically, a true Jedi housewife. "Goodbye" was all a bosomed Clerk would ever tell her girlfriends about those last, fleeing moments.

"Speak to me. Why do you never speak? Speak."
"What are you thinking of?"
"What thinking? Who thinks around here?"
"What? I never know what you are thinking. Think."
"Therefore, I am."
"Am not."
"Are too!"
"R too, D2."

I think we are in a run-down cemetery where dead men scavenge body parts from corpses untouched by heavy metal music.

"What is that noise down the hall?"
"Probably groupies."
"This is supposed to be a select, four-star hotel."
"The wind. . ."
"Exactly. You mean nothing?"
"Exactly. Exactly what I mean."
"Nothing?"
"Nothing."
"Nothing."

I remember the bags under her eyes.

"Are you alive, or not? Is there nothing in your head?"
"O O O O that Shakespearean Rag—It's so elegant."
"My mind is a mass of confusion."
"So intelligent."

"Oh that every marriage were made in heaven and moved as smoothly as Romeo and Juliet's less, of course, the two death numbers at the end."

"Of course. None pledge eternal love together, before the evening news ends anymore."

"Nothing pledged, nothing gained or dusted I always say."

"What shall I do now? What shall I do? Shall I rush out as I am, walk the street, and let all my hair down so or should I be what everyone wants me to be?"

"The glossies, the TV ads, the newspapers. The hot shower at ten. The 11 o'clock News, 10 Central Time."

"And if it rains, maybe I'll believe some weather reporter's stories. Others I won't."

"And shall we play another game of monopoly, pressing greedy eyes together and waiting for a ship to come in?"

"When Lil's first husband got divorced for the fourth time, I said— I didn't mince my words, I said to her myself . . ."

"HURRY UP ITS TIME TO GO TO THE BANK."

"Now Albert's being paroled and going to remarry the live-in roommate he spent the last six months with in the co-ed halfway house, after he got out the first time and made himself a bit smarter with refresher courses."

"He'll want to know what you've done with that money he gave you to get yourself educated."

"I did. He was there. Four years at a major university, Lil."

"And such a nice degree."

"He said," I swear, "I can't, I can't bear to talk to you."

"And no more can I," I said,

"And think of poor Albert, he's been at MIT four years now, he wants a good job."

"And if you don't give it to him, there's other's that will," I said.

"Now there," she said.

"Something about the Fortune 500 firms that might appeal to him," I said.

"Then I'll know who to go on about," she said.

"And give me a nasty look will ya. . ."

"HURRY UP ITS TIME TO GO SHOPPING."

"If you don't like shopping with me you can go wait in the atrium or the vestibule, if you prefer."

"Others can pick and choose if you can't marry the man," I said.

"But if Albert elopes, it won't be for lack of a best man."

"You ought to be ashamed," I said, "to talk so." (And him only thirty-something.)

"I can't help it," she said, pulling on her Maidenform.

"It's them books she reads from the publishers," I said. (She's read five already and nearly died of the last one when she listened to heavy metal records played backwards.)

"The feminist shrink said it would be alright, but I was never the same."

"You are the proper fool," I said.

"Well, if Albert won't leave you alone, there it is," she said.

"What did you get married for, if you don't want children?"

"HURRY UP ITS TIME TO DO MORE SHOPPING. SHOPPING."

"LADIES."

"Well, that Sunday while we were there, Lil had a hot one."

"And they asked me to leave them alone of course, to get about while their song was still playing."

"HURRY UP ITS TIME."

"HURRY UP ITS TIME."

"All the stores will close in a little while."

"Good night Bill. Goodnight Lou."

"Goodnight Ellie May. Good night."

"Ta ta."

"Good night. Good night."

"Sweet dreams. Good night."

"Good night shoppers. Good night. Good night sweet shoppers. Good night."

3. The Hired Demons

The river's course is broken: the last bulldozer clutches the ground and sinks into the wet bank of dirt. The wind crosses a brown land, unheard over the roar of many grinding diesels. The nymphs have started across the walk in front of the construction site. The men whistle to their sweet things ever so softly, 'til the contract ends. This water on-site shares empty Styrofoam, floated bottles, crumpled papers, worn rubber tires, foaming wastes, cigarettes or other testimony of Satan's fall. The nymphs are crowded at the bars. And their friends: the loitering heirs of city heat having left no phone numbers. By the waters of the sea I sat down and wept. . .

Fortune 500 poets travel so little through my house. Why am I so ugly to them, these sweet souls that run so softly along the roads they drive at night?

Am I so arrogant like a black bird picking a corpse scattered across the road, chased away by every car, waiting as long as possible to be carried away on its wings?

Write indoors in winter, exteriors in spring and summer and let autumn take its course. These are poetry's first rules of success, or is that excess? I think to not write them down anymore but instead, remember the changes in this day. I envision myself king of Fortune 500 poetics, lord of every yuppie lover's heart, the next Rod McKuen. Yet, I am negative and critical with multi-national implications, arrogant sometimes, and mostly withdrawn. Still, I remember the most positive emotions within myself and see all negative ones as chains yanked by spirits hiding in the shadows of night.

O the moon shone bright on the nymphs and her daughters: the Players that move too quickly on to the next poet. They wash their feet in rent-a-Jacuzzis, another idea past its prime. They wash their face in bubble gum.

Unreal, wasted land visited for the last time under a spiritual fog and a lusty, winter moon. The land once flowed with milk and honey. How to reconcile perfect choices?

Unshaven Einstein, with a pocket full of candy formulas shook the balance and opened up the military/industrial complex. A lush green haven of mind, body, and spirit turned intellect, turned away for answers. He who would not swallow a blue or red Quantum pill.

Now, once and for all, there is perfect hopelessness for one and all.

Lack of perfection leads intellect to justify imperfection at every picnic table by the roadway of life.

Turn upward from your tower where impressionable minds like fine-tuned racing machines, wait. I, middle-aged though bored, exist between eleven universes with a life busier than most, to sit behind a desk writing. And still, those eleven universes may have eleven dimensions. And so on it goes until I am an ascended particle master of all I survey.

I am with steroid breasts larger

than most skinny women's. I see past the happy hour. The evening hour promises bribes for those homeward angels held over in flights of rush-hour fancy and all that gives bartenders an extra hour's wage.

The gypsy sports hero, home during the off-season, lights the one bulb lamp above his bank statements. He lays out the product endorsements, the many contracts a sportsman is expected to hustle after a day's game. Anyone seeing the numbers would envy this ability to draw crowds.

I, a middle-aged old man with wrinkled toes from standing in the river of dreams too long, no longer living in the wasteland, perceived the scene, was still able to explain it. The muses still twist one arm behind my back and tie strings around all my fingers so I won't forget. (I expect no guests in a desert void of imagination, housing war castles of sand or mud.)

He, a young guitar repairman, arrived. A small businesswoman with one bold stare, one of the new nouveau, me—too so rich on whom name-dropping sits easily as a tenth-time hostess for the local fundraiser; the time now advantageous for foreplay, he guessed.

The microwave meal is ended. She is bored and tired, sitting cross-legged on the couch picking her teeth. He endeavors to engage her in a caress that is unreproved, unrequited. He assaults at once. Callused fingertips encounter no defense. His vanity requires no response and welcomes the hairy rankness of her indifferent, stale underarms and cigarette breath. (And I, a middle-aged old man, have been here before and left soon after. I, who have sat second row below Pink Floyd's wall of speakers, walked among the lowest of the undereducated dead, and lived to tell about it.)

And he bestows one final, patronizing kiss on her upper lip, asking himself what this woman does for him. She stares at the moment and into an aluminum pan reflection, hardly aware of her departed heavy metal husband. Her one remaining brain cell allows this thought to form: "He ain't no Valentino or rock music superstar." She thinks of needs and caring, paces the room alone, and never speaks of love.

The lovers glow with oil and ventilate, heating the beaches blushing with a turning tide of desire for a wild ride, a pure kiss on the lips where it counts, straight up and true, pure, once more from the heart.

Once more before I die.

Elizabeth and Leicester bring out the worst in each other and then rub the wrong way. She compares him to swollen flames and expects expectations—more true friends and family voices to flap at.

E&L play their games of chance and inspiration laughing, or trying patience laughing at all the time interwoven with love's most blissful spotlights; mostly doubting, still hoping perfection is like beautiful Cinderella and her fresh, Bel Air prince—too close for friendship, too unyielding to be soul mates; both with lovers and other internal scars only their egos see. They touch the wounds and then rub their eyes. Both desire change and never find time, time to talk the talk, thinking they've wasted or lost the years walking the walk.

4. Death By Intellect

"Why does the public wait until after the death of an artist or writer until he or she is discovered?"

"It has to do with the critics."

"They safely pick bones and theorize and then without fear of authoritative correction or contradiction."

Ah, the life of a critic. A critic's life, gentile or Jew, is one of air and expectations, except for the few exceptions. Only a university will take them in off the street and feed them.

5. *What the Shrink Didn't Say*

"Eat your peas," they both screamed at me.

"Interesting," he replied unemotionally.

"What's it mean though?" The patient sat up on the couch alert, in expectation of this, his final session.

"Very interesting your family life."

"What does it mean, Doc?"

"Your family was conservative was it not?"

"Yes, but what does it mean?"

"As a little boy this happened, yes?"

"Yes, yes. We've gone over that in detail."

"They always threatened to FedEx your dinner to all the starving children in China or Africa?"

"Yes, their words exactly."

"Interesting. I've never come across a case like this in all my many years of psychiatry."

"Ahhh. This is crazy. What is it?"

"Ah. Where's the time gone?"

"You're kidding?"

"Another day, another insight: that's my motto. Session's over."

"You're a fake."

"I would never tell anyone that, if I were you."

"I'm on the edge of a cure and you stretch it out one more session. You're crazy."

"Exactly my diagnosis. You're cured."

If nature were therapy and not rock? If there were rocks to stand on; and waterfalls; and water to catch us when we fall; a spring, a pool among the rocks to stand on and rinse off? If there were the sound of water only in this life? (Not the centipedes in the dry grass endlessly walking somewhere, walking; but the sound of water over a rock where the parrots mock from alloyed cages, "Polly is a Quaker. . .Polly is a Quaker.") But Mother Nature has no miracle cure.

Who is the third person of the trinity always beside you? When I count, there are only you and I together but when I look up Abbey Road there is always one walking beside you. I do not know whether a man or angel from our many conversations together. Quickly, who is that in the middle of the road, no on the other, other side trying to turn us just as we reach a crossroads?

What is that sound on Mother's Day? Murmur of maternal lamentation, the same hooded hordes of bomb threats swarming together over endless, useless pay phone wires, stumbling in temporal, earthen houses meditating on the missed card or Mother's Day gift.

Falling eardrums.

Jerusalem. Athens. Alexandria.

Nine out of ten therapists agree: "Don't repress feelings for your mother."

Batgirl drew her long, black hair tight and fiddled popular music for the MTV video. Bats with baby faces in the caving light whistled, beat their wings, and made their way to the corporate offices. All bats out of hell are sent by former songsters when play rotation of their tune is questionable, money runs out or songs peak too soon when a thousand voices imprisoned in empty cassettes and exhausted vinyl sleeves sit in warehouses waiting for discount auctioneers.

In this decayed denomination among the sidewalks in the moonlight, the choir is singing over the open graves about the chapel and empty pews. The sinners are all gone. There are no stained glass windows and the door swings on its hinges. Dry bones collected. In a flash of enlightenment the last member of the congregation falls asleep.

Ghandi's coffin was unearthed. Limp leaves were covered by dirt from the sunken-eyed diggers' shovels. Over distant chanting faces whispering crouched, breathing heavily, expecting silent nirvana.

Then spoke the thunder—

DUH

TA DA.

What have we forsaken?

Blood surrenders to spirit; the awful daring of a shaking heart in an age of impropriety. Depressed by this and this only, we have judged existence not found in obituaries yet to be written or under seven seals broken by the angels in their empty, little heads.

DA

DUH

TA DA.

I have heard the fighting between camps. Freud vs. Jung. Jung vs. Spock. Spock vs. the Clignons. Timothy vs. the dead Leary. And so on. By the way, he knocked at my window one night, soon after croaking, he being chased I think, by every spirit he seduced for eternity.

Turn the key once and turn once only.

One ping only before we defect to the other side, to capitalism, where democracy campaigns with the food that would feed the motherland all winter. We think of the key, each in his or her first person prison, turning the key.

He came to set the prisoners at liberty.

Turn
DA
key Spock.
DUH
TA DA.
Only at nightfall. Rumors spread.

Relive for a moment a heart broken for eternity.

TA DA.
TA DUH!

People just off the boat responded to the census. To the experts the sea was wet behind the ears and responses completely predicable, well within statistical probability and, if invited to the lottery, to obediently follow Big Brother's controlling hands.

I sat upon the throne looking down with a view through the clouds below me. With arid desert plains below I lean on higher ways not my own.

All the shrinks falling down, falling down, falling down; all the shrinks come falling down, my fair lady.

Like London Bridge in Texas, these fragments are stored in short-term memory, maybe for eternity.

I've left for the last time.

a morning glory
wraps its vines around a post,
purple flowers bloom

Transformation of the Ovary (into Fruit)

"Malus Sylvestrus, apple of the woods; Malus Pamila, small apple."

Rain watered my orchard until I found you:

an autumn apple:

split, filled with small, bitter seeds—
hard teardrops buried long before
gray winds became dark backhands
across the cheek of another day.

1. You sometimes speak of who
you've taken in—for apples; often,
needing up to three varieties for fertility;
those a father ignored.

You knew before we met there couldn't be
any more perfection. Unripe trees are felled
and burned by lovers already gone.

2. There are only leaves around you now—
leathery, elliptical and serrate. Like you,
they are bright, green, and smooth on top—

envied, constant; passed over by those
who ignore spirit, what you've been in gardens
of drying, tinted hair—leaves paler, more
dowry than skin beneath bright, open sunlight
where only gray shadows reach.

3. A glossy yearbook of schooled trees
tumbles from a dusty, open shelf
when I consider another.

4. This is what you are:

a blossom with limbs like stem petals:

ends or beginnings; seeds, or tomorrows—
that and what I already know—calyx like cotton
cooling an ovary, covering life always renewed;

like fingers beside style and stigma; a tree
with empty limbs overhanging a barren womb
easily opened; lines that have ended in neglect.

5. I once touched a white flower flush with pink
collagen—highlights of many winds; not who I am:

bark on arms grown from shaded, scaly thoughts
that bear the weight of many pomes.

After you've bled, you are what I am—
a spring: words like pollen, or a hand.

Toy Animal Time

Cloth lips like flowers and words like glossy rain—but not
all flowers fall on warm spring days; with raindrops wetting
plush toy animals strewn from a pickup across a back road.

Some dreams held tightly between arms fold into words—
flowers open and close in morning rains, on lips opening
and closing like pink flowers falling from dogwood trees.

Sometimes dreams rise from fields readied for planting;
though passing cars often ignore asides in rain; what spins
and stops—for I am falling and remember what has fallen.

I once fell beside flowers along city roads where animals
stuffed into metal donation boxes collect makeshift towns,
then fall on sand lots where dreams play out without words.

Evil Drives a Minivan

"Sometimes evil drives a minivan"
From the "Desperate Housewives" TV show.

Most "beautiful" people here drive minivans:

I know their souls have been sucked through their eyes
by alien beings more times than they care to admit; souls
frozen in time, doing too much suburban grilling. Dark
eyelids hide lost, cloudy-white eyes. Death drives a minivan.

They wear designer labels, watch Desperate Housewives,
Crossing Jordan and C.S.I. reruns on uber-duber stations.
Afterwards, they weave in and out of traffic or seasons
of success without knowing why. Death drives a green minivan.

Their eyes never look directly into the light, don't do evil,
and don't know why they spin news out of control,
in several counterclockwise directions—a life without surprise.
Death drives a slick minivan.

They flit from house to house, home to school,
to find the mall full of clothes they buy and return
again. They walk tile hallways like bingo players.
"BINGO!" Death drives a two-tone minivan.

Deadly hair in a tuss, that always needs repair; follicles parted in the middle like Moses tapping a Red Sea with a snake stick— a face framed with bleached headlights. Death drives a two-tone green minivan, slick, gassed, and ready to ride to town.

A Girl Covered in Forest

To a girl covered in forest:

brushed angora sweater and pants, like moss, camouflage
growing north on skin that disappears into the forest. Like
snails or butterflies, their touch of memory, their fingers
touching a memory of hands like snails or butterflies, unlike
winter and snow that melts in a day as they look into her eyes.

To a girl grinding spice:

in a cottage built on seven corners where seven roads meet,
passing ten kingdoms, each sitting on an ancient mountain
where height freezes snow and winds don't reach her. Time
blows at wooden doors, plank strips held fast with iron bolts
and hinges hammered into ancient stones for the end of days.

To a girl who makes bread on a common table:

she rises from the forest covered in dangled moss, to take
a bowl of flour to her kitchen. Bare feet perpetually slide
across the barren floor. She stuffs scavenged wood into an oven
and breathes on the dry fuel catching fire. Smoke vents
through the kitchen's roof as she breathes crude, common air.

She stirs flour, yeast, and wild grains, squeezing water
from the consecrated moss covering her. Kneaded dough rises,
warmed in one hand; in the other are spices she sprinkles.
She forms one loaf, sliding it into the heart of the oven,
jerking the bread from a paddle rubbed with flour.

Leaning the wooden paddle against the brick wall, she sails
a stick of incense into the crackling flames. Outside, smoke
mixes with forest air, wind blowing the thinning circle of offering,
the rising and falling scent of sustenance eventually covering
each of 10 kingdoms. She removes the bread.

Once more, the finished crust browns and she sucks in
the glowing coals, laying envy in its place; hanging
the paddle on the wall. She leans against a worn,
ancient tree to wait for him, her mouth a burning fire.

To a girl covered in moss in winter:

arms and legs spread like roots of a tree; a head of dark hair
and thin, dark shoulders bent against the trunk. Lean shadows
like flaking bark, like silent words spoken through her eyes,
through a mouth that never moves to flesh, only to spirit.

To a girl in winter:

a face with the tattered shadows of gray skies, half a forest
reflected in her eyes, and half of her story. She leans into
the clearing to hear shuffling leaves and tinkling metal.

Dark hair covers her shoulders hidden under hanging, dark
branches hung with covering chimes, earrings with golden bells
that reflect any shadowed light, like chimes. The metal wind
echoes in charmed rooms beside an ancient forest clearing,
a small, gold sound in a cold wind that dulls the whistling space
of her tiny room.

To a girl ungloved in winter:

hands, feet, and face like bare ground. He pulls off one glove
to still the chimes, to slay her music, to show her he's music;
the warm metal in his hand, a hand like a snail or a butterfly.

Her eyes open to his touch, too heavy or too quick from
a mountain covered with forests. He smells his harvest,
and one loaf still warm on the oven's ledge; moldy loaves
scattered on the one ledge around the entire room.

Broken leaves and sticks caught in the moss shade her
covered skin below the unclothed eye of the Cuba left behind,
that he's never seen; beaches overgrown with palms and brush.

A distant, equatorial sun still shines on Caribbean sand broken
off from continents risen from inside her, from molten flames,
cooling palms, and broken vines drawing the deepest secrets
from her Cuban blood. He quarters and breaks bread, pressing
one bite like a sacrament to her tongue. "This is their body,"
she says.

To a girl feasting on every forest sound:

of blood, flesh, and body consumed, flesh settling into white,
sandy beaches, a mother who mixes desire into flesh, bone,
and living water. She swallows the steamy flesh melting
on her tongue. He follows.

To a girl whose lips are open:

he rubs her lower back with one hand, moss warm to the touch;
barren skin like Angora, like spongy moss, tentacles breaking,
to fall where he lays, on bread fallen on the forest floor.

Her dark eyes hide burning her veins like lava rivers, hell
lain on top of a molten sea of forgotten sight. She looks to
the next traveler, past following incense through the woods
to anyone who lays like a mountain rising over a dry sea.

Snow-capped summits once frozen in place, snow hardened,
are packed down in storms reborn, that touch her now,
their waters melting as he bends to his moss forest.

He descends into a molten desert under her dark eyes, crusted
skin like baked bread, like fiery soil cooling in rain from snow,
from every mountain that falls into a forest.

She drinks kind, stolen waters, saying, "Bread eaten in secret
is pleasing, flour scraped and milled from their arms, legs,
and moist backs," the secrets of kings reborn inside her,
expired sweat that enriches the soil.

"I smelled the incense, the bread, and came," he says.
"Gather for me," she looks at the empty basket near the oven.

He does so because high winds no longer blow over his mountains,
his gift of pieces of broken wood become his dark frown.

She pulls a stick of incense from his marked brow; and why
he's here. Sweat pours from his frozen skin mixed with stolen
winds, winter's cold blowing through a cottage in the woods,
to an oven warming darkness under a forest's gray light.

The sweet smell of her skin reaches again, a forest of broken
oaks, poplars, and elms; the branches of a broken past placed in
her cooling oven. She lays the incense stick on the piled wood.

She touches the hand returned to her, warming his skin with
molten heat covered in moss. He places more bread in her mouth
and breathes deeply of the bread, spice, and perfumed oils,
to taste her burning tongue with his.

Unpainted lips, skin fragrant in falling rain releases his touch,
blood born of morning to sunset, until desire soaks her legs
tucked under the forest's blanket, under moss trees washed by
a cold mountain:

from being outside, behind her, washing her,
of being inside washing his back with oil from her hand.

Once, she licked salt from his arm, her first at the ocean,
inside her Cuban hideaway where he hid, pretending
there is distance between forests, between each king.

To a girl with aged wine in her eyes:

she drinks of his passion, wine washed down with dark eyes;
memories yielding colors to her wet lust becoming his coarse
spice, raw flour scraped from lovers releasing what ferments
in their hearts. Yeast and sugar powder, to dry on crude tables
others made in need of clearing, bare forest ground washed with
cold mountain tools, highlands crumbling in a day, flaked bark
peeling in time flaking his parting lips, the sweet fire and ice
of maturity; age cooling in each other's arms.

To a girl who smiles in pooled rainwater:

who bathes with him in winter's slow fingers, in rainwater
dripping from hair to those who drink her wine.

She mentions a king, her first. Jealous, he accuses her
of allowing them to eat at her table; floors wetted with snow
falling from clouds covering many mountains, drops of
beading water toweled dry with the damp moss of wet,
excess skin that opened her forest.

To a girl in a forest cottage who never leaves:

lashes never running with tears, eyes unteared in cold wind.
He lies with her, with her fire until his heart no longer beats,
blood boiled away, evaporating with their sins still inside him,
air becoming blood or smoke, settling coals where seven roads
meet, where kings will taste her lips again.

She grates his skin and bones and more spice from his brow.
Sharp, scooping nails, like honed spoons, spade what flour
missed the bowl. She scrapes yeast and wild grains from
her own skin, some dark dust falling into the moss.

Angels, Pearls and Mannequins

"Neither cast ye your pearls before swine,
lest they trample them under their feet. . ." Matt 7:6

Each New Year I stop by family graves
asking for ease, as if anything they could do
would put me on track; and then I drive south:

there, a half-moon, slightly less really, was a half-buck
short of a dollar. I thought today would become warmer
and make up the difference. There, I would hammock
under heaven:

arms stretched back behind my head, gazing
at clouds moving across the face of a broken moon
on a black Formica sky.

When I needed truth you were honest:

but there's distance between us. Every day you slip
more new clothes over pearl-dusted mannequins
in window displays.

You may have forgotten I took you graveside first:

where you were afraid, as we turned into the cemetery.
Behind that wall nothing moves or speaks. I spoke,
as if spirit never dies, when angels easily move
the darkness aside. There, with the angels,
I saw you for the first time.

In the morning clouds fell across the sun:

an eye opening once more to a sky not holding
my attention. Like winter birds gesturing south
your perfume lingered on my shirt.

You once gave me jewels.

The Center of the Universe

Behind,
thick stones are colder, deeper than time emptied,
poured into each moment that passes between clouds
that eventually disappear on the horizon.

Shadows on darkness fall from the mountains:

the sacred moving slower than geologists say,
as we turn to the bright autumn air.

(Clouds fall even in darkness.)

Under each rising sun, when there is no darkness; still—
they've always fallen. When there are shadows they fall again:

today; on the ground with less space for the sun or moon.

Before you left falling behind, before you left falling
from them, sounds always fell behind the horizon:

what is lowest behind each forest;
like trees circling the imperfect edges of me,
fallen;
touched.

There, I hear a voice before I was made, before midnight
when the universe of blue spaces between clouds of importance
closed; space you ran to seeking another new moon, or sun;
or sky with horizons closer to the center of the universe.

In seeking the center,
the blue spaces of universe first;
first:

there is no mountain,
then there is;
then there is no mountain.
(I've heard my heartbeat there.)
Then there is.

If there is darkness, you will know. If there is darkness
in the stillness between shadows falling across these mountains
I already know.

The Ferryman's Opera

Thick, woven dreams are stitched
in gold or silver thread, or a touch
of distance cooling under her robe.

His opera is less now, crossing
the river, subtitled with legs crossed;
legs covered in more, brighter colors.

He listens to her voice one shadow
at a time, the distance of words
in half-time, pairs folded each dawn.

In the morning she opens the window
and wakes to shoes rumbling over
the poured stone roads.

Distance sits on the gray-brown steps
above the street outside:

her skin covered under illuminated oils
after a day baking in clear sunlight.

Her eyes close under fingers pressed
like death coins saved for the ferryman,
faceless value dipped in rising inflation,
costing more than their worth to mint;
his journey no longer threatening.

Her cheeks are hallow near a mouth
spread with moist, colored gloss:

shine evaporating in the hot, damp air;
hands and arms weighed in each touch,
fingertips on fingertips merging in traffic.

Once more, the ferryman whispers nothing
vital carrying him across the River Styx.

Spirits from a Bamboo Grove

"Bamboo represents creativity and innovation."

1. A bamboo grove encircles a house
in the middle of a six-stringed city:

a cottage holds her shingled heart
rummaged where her men still lay.

One says, "I never chose this." She says,
"I accepted your every word for what it was."
He says, "Nothing is more important than this."
Nothing.
For a year.

2. Cellphone to one ear she finds
her face from bathroom trays,
instant breakfasts, and pregnant smiles.

She offers her cheek; but now
he weighs more than her forgiveness.

3. A child in the grove is born
from a woman's jasmine-scented temple

and oak doors that will never open again.
Without a uterus her walls have tumbled down
to become Crayola gods.

4. They run across carpets that are rivers.

5. She passes crowds hiding behind
clogged skylines of rush hour traffic
slowing for afternoon lights.

Her dense, ancient horizon is bitter with
the cold, ungargled taste of the winter
he left behind.

6. She desires fiery solitude for her work:

straightforward wealth to rude nothingness.

7. Since the grove burned an awareness
settles into her spirit:

her art, less than his, becomes mornings
that are gray again.

But that was long ago. She says, "It's difficult
to believe it's been seven years." He says,
"Now, clouds of evergreens are our muse."

Dark Pursuit

Night:

a car approaches from behind. Laughter
and rusty springs ride squeaky rhythms around a curve.
Headlights sweep the forest followed with a ghostly exhaust.
Red stars sneak 'round two-lane corners without staring.
The smoke drifts on the pavement as pale figures
behind the wheel disappear over and down a hill.

Sunrise:

warm and cool shadows hug the edge of the highway.

Dodging Potholes:

cool air under the forest rolls the median dust.
Maple leaves tumble like cards, landing on upstairs windowsills.

Dusk:

midriff clouds hang over the rails of November's belted fields.
Winter is close.
Steel air rusts below a low, damp sun peering through

the blue-gray sky.
There are more colors beside the powdered road.

Orange:

I've forgotten her words.

Black:

leaves disappearing under a passing car.

Brown:

leaves before mulching moral equivalents.

Yellow:

leaves cooler to the touch than the sun's haze.

Red:

leaves on fire without smoke.

Green:

what remains of a day.

Tonight:

the orange sin of a rising moon
hides behind trees neither full nor bare.
Leaves caught by dark, pursuing waters drift downstream.

Screw Most, If Not All MFA Programs

"And he that falleth on this stone shall be broken to pieces: but
on whomsoever it shall fall, it will scatter him as dust." Matt 21:44

i

I close my eyes to moonlight,
to days trained by suns setting,
after each day is traced by more suns,
as every shadow turns to stone,
where I am a stone of empty space,
as I become a sword again:

a white sword of empty space,
the bright white sword
between pages of emptiness,
between the empty lines of your emptiness,
the thin space of lines between empty books
filling your dusty, wooden shelves,
in books once flesh and blood.

You bathe the world in mediocre thoughts,
in the clean, running water of mediocre thinking;
in swirling,
draining water
falling into unclean holes,
mediocre thoughts running to unclean exams.

I rise in the yeast of heartbeats:

in heartbeats between your legs, behind each breast,
and in breasts beating with the illusion of time's full breasts,
time's broken breasts toasted in crisp moonlight;
microwaved time in the garbage-fed stream of evening news;
of evening fat chewed during the evening news;
of bacon fat chewed each morning, noon, and night.

You chew and swallow heartbeats like breasts; like porn;
like chicken fingers swallowed whole; with porn-dipped sauce
licked from chicken fingers between sips of fine-ground coffee.

You chew imported eggs with instructions seated at a diner
in moonlight, where moonlit students serve bacon and eggs
in all-night diners until they close their eyes to mediocrity.

In closing my eyes to the moon I remember all moonlight
and forget the same moment of breath taught in school—
the living, breathing, dying breath of recess, of red rubber balls
bounced against wire-glass doors, steel inset
with giggling, wire-glass moonlight, of red balls kicked
into the outer space of wire-glass stars picked first in hallways
where death never runs and always walks single file;
red rubber balls sent to orbit just outside the rusted steel doors
of the last day before Christmas break.

Christmas starlight spins on frozen trees, on Christmas,
in Christmas tree darkness once I hit the ball and ran each base
from here to there with my dad chasing me; racing the moon
and back again.

Now, only black shadows of red mica dirt cling to my shoes,
to the bottom of my black, low-cut All Stars,
squeaking black tennis shoes squeaking on polished tile floors,
my impressions digging into the sparkling red clay like pollen,
like pollen filling the unglued bottom of gray soles,
like untenured, gray souls waiting for the free ride through time,
space, and every yard in between a gray and white sidewalk
of every afternoon alone.

Putting on new shoes I close my eyes to midnight
and walk the straight line back to school:

before midnight when I remember the short span
of light years ahead and leaving one second after midnight;
to have one second more to dance and spin;
and leaving one second after midnight;
to have that one second back,
to have one second more to spend looking back
at one second more, looking back just one second more;
to have eternity looking back at one second after midnight;

to have exactly one second more before you say
the one second after midnight is the same as the one second
before a morning sun rises and any day becomes another,
at dawn,
and not before;
and not one second more;
and not one second before I stare into the white fire of the sun
and not look away;

and not look away from the bright white stone of eternity
one second away,
and not look away from the bright white light of eternity
one second away;
one second away from every wish you've ever made:

one second away from white marble angels,
one second away from white fire made from black flint;
from white light; from white light one second away,
one second away from white fallen angels, falling angels
made of white light falling into black holes at the end of every star;
of every eternity for black holes falling into themselves forever;
one second away from white fire exploding; one second away
from white marble angels standing in the stone-cold moonlight.

Mannequins in a Perfect World

On soft chairs they wait. Dark strands
of unwashed vinyl hair; clean follicles strung
with gold, a color in every woman's eyes.

Empty light fades in worn cloth under hands
on arm rests woven with time unraveling:

a fleshy palm hidden when a woman is unsure.

Ebony and bronzed shoulders touch all faces,
more shadows; eyes plunging from unchanging
gazes from inside a hard plastic shell.

In a perfect world they wear other shadows
falling across storefront windows; glass souls
tinted for UV diversity.

Long legs rhyme with yesterday, as in pink is
the new black.

They walk black streets. Without white children
their taut bellies feed dark wombs.

The Signs of Water

Clouds are signs for all water:

today's wind blows them into frayed ribbons,
winter rippling the sky as it begins and ends.
I gather horizons for wonder, seeking
the comfort of distance easily seen.
Under a forest of leaves, looking around,
autumn is left under the trees, along
a sun-covered road by a river of clouds.
Still, the leaves flutter and shade
the reigning light, as do trees:

one sign that brings me to this mountainside
with the other 5000 who eat the broken fish
and leavened meal, to become like Him
each time I taste the bread and drink the wine,
to become the clear sky of winter; confessing
covenant, after taking my sins against others
to them and asking for their forgiveness.
Signs, like clouds, are washed away
like autumn leaves that point downstream.
Each color was once a sign of winter to come.

Shadows of Eternity

After Out of the Grey's, *Winter Sun*

Remember the ocean's stillness on rainy days
or the smoke of prayers smaller than
harvest fields or hands lacking oil or wine?
Starlings harvest this day's swirling excess,
in the highest trees scraping daylight threaded
through the fluttering distance, through a past
altered with windows crowded with plants.
The grayest thoughts drift to desire,
or every light without conditions.
Waiting for a winter sun, I find a midnight sky
carries the sparkling snow; gray shadows
that fall in the lucid moonlight.
Looking up, the snow floats down
between memories drifting in from the tree line,
far above where I first became winter,
as the first snow fell for a child wearing
excess clothes that always touched the ground.
(Such is the power of nature without Him.)
Circling branches balance rounded limbs
where sprawled snow breaks away
and shivers across the chilled earth.

Ground unburied in spring has its terms but,
too often, winter is taller than any street or town.
(In time, snow closes a city.)
But you are winter, the white flesh of eternity,
frozen rivers from clouds tipped to icy winds,
and larger than snow falling on this evergreen.
The nearby haze becomes more snow settling
on the dull forest darkness brightened by the
whitest daylight all year—brown bark that will be
bleached pure in the smallest shadows of eternity.

Under a Colored Sky

(For BWF on our 4th Wedding Anniversary)

Under the shadows is light where I stood before we touched,
under shadows that were never seen before. I could not say
hidden because we had not met the darkness, shadows
walking in rooms with eyes closed, alone:

whispering words that do not touch shadows or light;
sounds that never leave the spoken darkness; whispers
that are always shadows.
The sun is color to single source leaves, color from all light
given over shadows that disappear whenever you are light
inside me, under the colored sky where we dream—under
heaven—under God who is light that has no turning, above
the gray of everything else.

Valentine Secrets

(For My Wife)

Our secrets make us who we are:

dew settling on raindrops on a foggy, Valentine
Monday; a light of dawn in each eye as you wake
from holding night inside. Now, you hold mornings
in your dreams, kiss sun and stars on the lips,
faces with red hair and smiles, and hold their hands
to pray.
The wind whispers words only you and the trees
know to say; (our children will follow). It's not a song
but moments our hearts touch what is deepest:

painting words on green canvas skies, brown trees
drying under yellow, acrylic suns; the space
we share when sleds of time reveal each secret
that brought us here, across the broad street
of a lakeside paradise, or across a table of bread
and wine where moments disappear and heaven
is nearest to our hearts.
After the harvest of all hearts, we will say

"It is no mystery why we love as we do
and are loved as we are; His light creates
all light and each morning is renewed."

The Nature of Seagulls

A gray morning falls to the ground

night's darkness bends to a generous forest,
as stars gather winter again. Fluttering clouds
of seagulls descend on fields beside my home—
the sun rises over all fallen men.

Dawn spills over the edges of what is blinding,
what first brought us here, to an ocean circling
in clouds overhead; seagulls turning right,
back towards the sea, towards heaven.

They've taken leftovers from tractored fields
turned under metal plows before planting, family
drifting to harvest winds. Origination shows
intention, bringing destination closest.

I escape what's fallen away, middle grounds
taken. Still, gravity pulls from its past,
from the cool stillness covering spring's
woven fields.

A Church of Days

(For Leigh)

Twilight falls where church reflected on your eyes:

ancient light, pure beginnings; first opened to fade
as they closed their heart to what follows, when their eyes
revealed encircling light that is neither dark nor light;
souls covering you with seeds from a forest encroaching
the fallen city.

They've planted before, when you first closed your eyes,
where spirit never dies. Their eyes close, dimmed each time
they sew their light. Under your eyelids are stars remembered,
guides to ancient paths where no one runs. They see
fertile earth and a sparkling river.

Twilight falls on the river until both disappear
in small, quiet waves soaking the damp sand;
bright earth from dust speaking to ancient shores
washed of thought. Once before, they opened
their eyes and covered you with stars.

Once they covered you with stars you became a bearer,
as they are bearers of light years ago. Only clay
and blood are left behind now—what a hard, bare river
runs to when storms fall back into the black river.

Your eyes open to a church of sand and sea,
the dimming light of time and oceans you hide
in a church of days washing you with gray
and blue midnight falling into more days of the same
pampered loam; seeds grown on red and green horizons.

Waves of twilight roll over brief winds rushing home
before the dry light disappears into another complaint,
where starlight sits around a table on stiff, creaking chairs,
feeding you more seeds for each meal, before
the city opens its eyes again.

Islands of Eternity

Broken sand and shells disappear under a frayed, capped ocean:

smooth-edged clouds shade cypress trees from the sun,
as endless seams of waves float ashore.

I hold dull berms or seeds to bury in the loam—
washed in the afternoon; screened dark clouds
hover over the wave-lined ocean.

A cloud is only water risen.

I am water and desire to be a cloud again;
drifting in wind blowing tomorrow's waves
over shadows that settle between waves
and the time it takes to return.

For sand:

there are only waves of white and gray water,
footprints or the sun.

A Season of Angels

Morning is still.

From the beginning shadows of harvest moons
are longer than the waiting for dreams to gather
like this dew. A long, harvest night comes and goes
with its promises of the year to come from a season past:

when we were given to each other, before we met
in the afternoon. Then, night birds, asleep or dreaming,
were awoken by machines like sickles and trucks,
like people hiking to the ripening fields.

I can no longer carry what you must carry yourself
through the harvest, alone, by machines. Gathering
is life; and friends. Night birds sang through the strain,
melodies we shared and gave words; a blue moon rose
and fell on every note taken from the earth, given
to the sky.

Morning birds fly over the flattened fields strewn
with debris, seeking life uncovered by time,
what was planted before; what memories or crumbs
we are made of. The sun rises again, over horizons,

clouds, and time; more than dreams or memories,
more than we touched alone.

We turn from the rows cut by tires of harvest wheels,
flattened before the spring rains, and what you take
to heaven. Morning is still again, for the instant we look
into each other's eyes; a long, harvest night come
and gone with its promise of this moment.

Uncut Maps

After a "Postcard of Valentine, Nebraska"
by Dunlap-Henline Distributors (c.1960)

1. Flowers fall on sparse grass:

spring's early flowers bud between a mild now
and a cold winter stalled inside cares. They push
against the blurred murmurs of glass speculation
to the patchy dirt around a greenhouse.

Green azalea leaves shade hidden branches—more flowers
hiding under the young shade of spring covering each afternoon
of chores; pool hustlers good enough to walk alongside a long row
of bushes near a street close to TV fame.

2. Uncut thoughts edge through reinforced doors, pool players,
as the convenience store empties before a small town tournament—
a dollar a game, four quarters in silver then, into the belly
of one of two beefy slate tables; not the pro tables I remember
from high school.

The bowling alley then, the occasional home for sportless teens:

buying cigarettes underage at a chest-high machine for
thirty-five cents each, a dime more than the drug store;
the machine next to the back door; forty packs wide,
as wide as the alley's entire forty lanes. We nervously
slot coins to play one or two games of pool.

3. Outside:

miracles from manufactured fertilizer pads layered under
threaded roses tracking the length of the plastic house.
Thick, brushed carpets; worn fibers like red azaleas
past indifference.

4. Inside:

a paneled wall separates glossy, maple boards
and slate tables I bowed to most Saturdays:

the rolling, pounding plastic of all colors constantly popping
the white pins. With a perfect roll all pins slide, dungeon swept;
like pool balls spun into woven leather string pockets;
the clicking energy of ivory balls bouncing off the brick walls
of brief distractions from the abyss around me.

Later, outside light dims. Fluorescent tubes brighten
the Saturday night pool tables; after bowling—each player
an island of angles like the moon's reflection of the sun.

A Hurricane Season

"To whom is reserved the blackness of darkness forever" Jude 13

All shadows are gray as I wait out this storm.
Thunder causes me to look inward, between
shadows where earlier there was light.

Night has fallen as at other times; mostly without rain.

Winds give way through trees where character
stops to look, asking if I believe spirits walk across
shadowed walls, if I should ever see them again.

You wear humid summer like a sticky T-Shirt.

Thick gray clouds swirl desire. Low riding radio bands
push blue skies north of easy listening. A blue-gray smoke
curls from chrome tailpipes. Whirling clouds of waves
circle the ocean, always waiting behind dull white cool;
the darkness hiding the rage. Tail-fire shoots into the night
as drivers gun engines. A line of storms shoots from
a starting gun, as if hurricane seasons are sanctioned
NASCAR races.

The phone call was out of place, late last night—distracting my introspection, briefly unbalanced with unseen thoughts from diversion. Unseen, more so than when reading the sky like a magazine, turning pages of what is eternal, more than when I'm alone.

A House of Rising and Falling Suns

Here, east meets west and north the south
where I am still, where I am never alone.

The gray does not leave; moisture
chilled with swallowing morning clouds
pinned under the sun. Before noon the fog
burns off.

Sometimes, afternoon is a busy town. I cross
a dark sky, an unarmed day when a man rides by,
past caring, who talks to himself. He pulls a knife
from a pocket, as I speak of a city never needing light.

Later, the gray returns with the evening news,
skies that turn back to morning when I started.

A Letter to Delilah

The car horn on the road woke me:

more than moonlight on water.
I am a mirror to you . . . and you of me . . .

In that dream I am calm; walking, turning
a road, along a field where I ask a Philistine,
as if I am Samson and you Delilah, "What
becomes green to gold and green again?"

Gold is yellow—distance mixed with brown
when eight colors challenged more than
sixty-four crayons and a sharpener placed
in small hands. Pieces of orange suggest rain;
or plans being disrupted.

Yellow in every poem is golden hair; the growl
of tawny lions; saffron flowers, bumblebees
or a brazen sun. Now you know what I know.

It's not cobalt blue so much I lack with weather
or age; colors are stolen each day; it's that police
never question a white haze gone missing,

uncolored after it settles in a hammock
between trees while other, uncolored pages
beg for attention.

But I am not Samson, nor you Delilah:

a golden mane grayed, blown thin. You seek
a coloring book of tinted meadows with
money trees growing beside a yellow brick road
of predictable, emerald towns.

We always walk into the cloudy breath
of suggestions on winter mornings;
small clouds like horizons spread across
fields waiting to become green.

One Explanation for Divorce

Intent desires more:

weddings of spirit and flesh, with hope clinging midair
to promises fingering the full lips of any dream come true.

Possibilities peddle against the headwind
of the genuine coasting downhill.

Desire spins thin tires of doubt
or thoughts buried deep within the heart:

strings of songs as deep as self, for the moments
longing lasts; when you listened, your mind made up.

With any indifference you stop for change; staring
at your phone, before words stall in situation,
distraction or intent. You were spirit once, untouched,
until I touched you. And now you are no longer my flesh.

But death is relative:

a slipping away of days no longer explained.

Road Trip

I never miss summer:

days when heat lingers past dusk,
as the worn, picnic grass cools until morning.
A shower follows the winding road; memories
turn from what doesn't grow in the gray light.

From the rain:

enter leaves falling where trees begin,
a brief cloud of time climbing a sky
of all colors, or all colors on the ground;
or shade where summer breathes softest.

At home, clouds cover the distant trees
and the gray is closer to the mist.

Self-Made Self

Haven't been here today:

a cool green world, the spring of what is left,
that leaves again under the deep soil of any moment.
But today is like any other day—before summer follows
with its burning gaze.

The heat of indifference rides up and down Main Street
when their obsession cools shopping all day with coupons,
bargain hunters who sit together at lunch; a familiarity
sipping iced relief. Glances turn at the same pace, focus
on the same thing; sit in the same chair each time.

Contentment shifts its view in windows reflecting the wavy mirrors
of self-made self; reason that has no reason to shift from view,
inside greetings that sound full of pretense. Those
with secrets walk past without a word, abruptly edging
around those who already know.

New Worlds in Moments

Broken tides move south today:

against winds slower than a sky crossing a beach, sands
touching the bending toes of age. But I am ageless like clouds
curving the horizon, touching the sea sometimes when it rains.

The sky's distance moves again, as stars cross heaven. Stars,
slower than eternity, count a billion years again and again,
in light becoming time and place, curving waves that shake
curling walls of predictability draining the salted shoreline.

The salt feeds everything:

gnarly pines, browned grass, the treated wood of tomorrow's decay.

Now, I am a farmer, reaping every moment:

earth and sky; flesh and bone, the contention of pebbles migrating
along the open cuts of shells on vacation. Salt heals everything.

Winds blow against tides, at angles changing with sunlit sand
never touching any waves. I daydream:

time weighs more than my spring seeds.

Every day is birth. What is not sound—stops. As the winds
roll the salt air over morning the sun spills on the ocean
and another day begins.